Sarah Leavitt

Tangles

A story about Alzheimer's, my mother, and me

Jonathan Cape

London

Published by Jonathan Cape 2011

2 4 6 8 10 9 7 5 3 1

First published in Great Britain in 2011 by
Jonathan Cape
Random House, 20 Vauxhall Bridge Road,
London SW1V 2SA

www.vintage-books.co.uk

Addresses for companies within The Random House Group Limited can be found
at: www.randomhouse.co.uk/offices.htm

The Random House Group Limited Reg. No. 954009

A CIP catalogue record for this book is available from the British Library

ISBN 9780224094221

The Random House Group Limited makes every effort to ensure that the papers used in its books are
made from trees that have been legally sourced from well-managed and credibly certified forests.
Our paper procurement policy can be found at: www.randomhouse.co.uk/paper.htm

Printed and bound in Great Britain by the MPG Books Group, Bodmin, Cornwall

For my father Robert and my sister Hannah.

For my dearest companion Donimo and my drawing friend Mary,
because I would never have finished this without you.

Most of all, for my mother Midge, whom I will miss forever.

Introduction

I've always had a really bad memory. So when my mother got Alzheimer's disease, I knew that I had to record what was happening to her and to our family. I wanted to be able to look back over my notes and remember all the moments of craziness, beauty, and tragedy—and not lose any of them.

Mom started showing symptoms of Alzheimer's in 1996, when she was only 52. Our family ran through all the possible explanations—job loss, depression, menopause—until finally we realized it must be something neurological. She was diagnosed with Alzheimer's in 1998. For the next six years my father cared for her, eventually with the help of hired caregivers. Mom's sisters, Debbie and Sukey, and my sister Hannah and I helped as much as we could.

I lived in Vancouver and my parents lived in Fredericton, New Brunswick. I visited two or three times a year, and took notes and drew pictures the whole time I was there.

I often felt like Harriet the Spy, or, in darker moments, like a vulture hovering and waiting for Mom to say or do something that I could record and preserve, even as she slipped away from me. Sometimes she would pull on the page or grab my pen as I tried to write. The pen would skid and make a mark and I'd label the mark: "Mom moved my pen." I wanted to keep every trace of her.

I ended up with a box of notes and sketches, some careful and considered, some dashed off in the middle of a crisis and barely legible or blotched with dried tears. There are small notes I made on scraps of paper right as things were happening, like at the dinner table when Mom started talking to the broccoli.

During Mom's illness, I started using some of my notes to write stories and essays about what was happening. I imagined writing a book. About nine months after Mom died I went through the journals, sketchbooks, and scraps of paper I'd collected over the six years of her illness. I chose a small number of drawings and notes, compiled them into a booklet, and made a few colour copies. I realized that instead of writing prose about my mother I wanted to do a graphic memoir, and I spent the next four years writing and drawing this book.

My mother loved her family with a fierce and absolute love. Alzheimer's disease tore her away from us and from herself in a cruel, relentless progression of losses. But even as she lost her ability to form sentences, and stopped saying our names, and stopped understanding ideas like sister, daughter, or husband, she would still cry out with joy when we came into the room.

I created this book to remember her as she was before she got sick, but also to remember her as she was during her illness, the ways in which she was transformed and the ways in which parts of her endured. As my mother changed, I changed too, forced to reconsider my own identity as a daughter and as an adult and to recreate my relationship with my mother.

This is the story that I have pieced together from my memories, my notes, and my sketches. Other people in my family may remember things differently. In the end, this is only my story: the tangled story of my mother, and me, and Alzheimer's.

Sarah Leavitt
Vancouver
March 2010

Part One

Nightmares

When I was little, we lived in the country in an old rented farmhouse. I slept upstairs at the back of the house in a creaky bed that the owners had left behind. The flowers in the wallpaper changed shape at night. Rats and squirrels ran up and down inside the walls.

Evil creatures lurked under the bed, so I couldn't get out unless I kind of jumped away from the bed.

I never forgot the chapter in Little House on the Prairie where a mouse chews off some of Pa's hair. I buried myself under the covers until I fell asleep.

But then the nightmares started. A robber caught me. Or a Black Rider. Or a Flying Monkey.

Aaaah!

I'd wake myself up screaming.

MOM!?!

And then I'd wait...

MOM

to be rescued.

ZZZZZ

MOM!

Z-

My mom was like Miss Clavel in the Madeline books, waking up in the middle of the night.

Aaah!

And I was Madeline, and something was not right.

Miss Clavel ran so fast down the hall that her body got all stretched out.

THUMP! THUM

I'd listen for the sounds of my mother's footsteps coming towards my room.

MOM? HELP!

When she got to my room I would pretend to be asleep so that she would have to wake me from my nightmare. She would sit on the bed and she was heavy and real and I knew I would never be scared again.

It's OK, honey. It was just a dream.

COMING!

I had nightmares right through high school. She always ran to me when I called her.

Years after I had left home and moved across the country, I had a strange nightmare.

My mother was floating away from me. She was wearing a long nightgown and she seemed confused. I woke up crying but she wasn't there.

Sisters

Mom was born in Poughkeepsie, New York in 1944.

She was the youngest of three sisters: Deborah, Susannah, and Miriam. They all had three-syllable names because their parents thought that sounded better with their one-syllable last name, Stone. Everyone called them by their nicknames, though: Debbie, Sukey, and Midge.

1944

Greetings from the Stones 1945

Love, the Stones 1948

Happy Holidays

Stone Girls '58

I only know a few stories about each of Mom's parents. Joe was a child psychologist who taught at Vassar.

He had also done some work with war veterans, and had somehow ended up with a box full of chewed-up razor blades. Supposedly a soldier chewed them.

When Mom was little, he took his family to a jazz club and they met Duke Ellington.

In 1965 he went to Selma and joined the marchers.

Beatrice, known as Bea, was a kindergarten teacher. She was fiercely loving and also tough.

We have a photo of her sitting on a dock somewhere in the 40s or 50s, wearing pants, looking ready for anything. One of her nicknames was Butch.

Once, when Mom was in her mother's class, a bad kid tried to take advantage of the situation.

Are you going to let me do it or am I going to have to hit Midge?

Neither one! And don't even think of trying that again!

Bea died of cancer when Mom was just 18. On her death bed she told Debbie to take care of little Midgie.

Mom's mother died just before Mom left for her first year at university. She told me and my sister Hannah that she got a private room so that she could cry as much as she needed to.

Joe died 12 years later, also of cancer. He felt horrible about making his children go through another cancer death. I was six, but I don't really remember him.

Orphan

In the field of sunshine was the first time
You tore apart my world with a word.
As the bright grass swam, dotted with daisies,
And the earth smelled so sweet
You went on telling, gentle, relentless.
The sun kept on shining
While cancer grew inside my mother.

When I was a teenager I found a poem Mom had written about her parents dying.

No matter how much time went by, Debbie, Sukey, and Midge talked and cried about their parents as if they had just recently died.

Debbie moved to a small town not far from Poughkeepsie. She lived with her son in a tiny house.

Mom ended up in the country in Maine, and eventually moved to Canada.

Sukey moved to Philadelphia with her husband.

They were all teachers. Debbie taught at an alternative school.

Sukey taught preschool.

Mom taught kindergarten like her mother had.

The sisters saw each other often. They would kiss and hug and retreat into their own world, where they talked about their parents and sang for hours in three-part harmony: folk songs, children's songs, Christmas carols (they were Jewish but definitely not religious).

John Henry was a little baby Sittin' on his daddy's knee

But the banks are made of marble, with a guard at every door and the vaults are stuffed with silver

Children go where I send thee! How shall I send thee?

They all sounded exactly alike on the phone.

Hello, Sarah darling!

They were so close.

There was one story about one of them hitting another one with a hairbrush at some point when they were kids.

 OW!

But that was the exception. The sisters never seemed to get mad at each other or even disagree.

One summer, when I was 13 and my sister Hannah was 11, Mom was at her wit's end.

We talked back all the time.

We left huge messes everywhere.

And we fought almost constantly.

YANK!

The three sisters remembered everything in detail, people and places and stories from decades ago.

Hannah was like that too.

Remember when we were at that party when you were in grade 12 and that thing Joanne said to Cathy about her dress and then remember what Cathy said back? Come on, yes you do! It was so funny!

Mom and Dad moved from Cambridge to Philadelphia to a small island in Maine, where I was born in 1969. In 1970 they moved to Boston, where Hannah was born.

Then we moved back to Maine for eight years in one town...

and two in another.

And then Canada, for a year in Cape Breton...

before we finally settled in Fredericton, New Brunswick.

My own memory was full of holes. Maybe it was because we moved so much.

When we moved to a new town, Hannah made friends quickly. She'd just get on her bike and go meet people. I hid inside.

One time Mom got so sick of me staying inside and crying that she tried to pull me outside with her when she went to run errands. I just refused to move and she finally gave up.

Eventually I made some friends, but Fredericton never felt like home. I couldn't imagine staying there. As far as I could see, there was only one possible future there, and I didn't want it.

I left as soon as I could, right after high school graduation.

Hannah went away to university but moved back in with Mom and Dad when she graduated.

We were very different.

I've been getting in touch with my Jewish heritage.

We're not really Jewish! Mom and Dad aren't religious!

This is the 90s! Own your power as a woman!

I know he's not very nice to me, but he's really hot!

I'm so depressed about the state of the world. I just can't bear it.

God, you are so dramatic!

And we were also very similar.

Mom? Are you awake? I need to talk!

Mom? Are you awake? I'm so upset!

I can't believe he said that! What an idiot!

Ah ha ha! I know!

Hannah and I weren't a unit like Mom and her sisters. In my mind, there was me and then the rest of my family, who I missed and felt liberated from at the same time.

Long Distance

After I graduated from university, I moved to Vancouver. I had a boyfriend, but things were beginning to fall apart with him. Right away I got involved in feminist activism.

Mom! My new friends are so amazing! And you know what? A lot of them are lesbians... I think I might be one too.

You know, sweetie, I've always thought that someone who had to go through a "coming out" process would end up being a pretty together person. You might not be a lesbian. Maybe you just have some really neat friends who you like an awful lot.

Oh. I never thought of that. Maybe you're right.

afghan that Mom knitted me →

By that point I'd decided that I did want to be a lesbian, so Mom's theory worried me. But then my boyfriend moved out.

beep! beep!

And soon after that I started dating women.

Mom! Dad! I have something important to tell you. I'm a lesbian!

That's great, honey. But didn't you already tell us?

Yeah, I think she did.

The whole coming out thing was pretty anticlimactic.

Hannah took it a little harder.

No you're not a lesbian. You had a boyfriend!

But are you sure?

Soon she got used to it, though.

So did you end up making out with that girl at the bar? Is she pretty?

Over the years we all got used to living on opposite sides of the country. Mom kept writing me letters every week, with news about the family, the garden, the kitty, and her work, and sweet notes about keeping my spirits up.

Dad wrote to me too, usually little random notes at the end of Mom's letters.

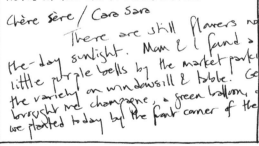

We talked on the phone every Sunday and sometimes more often.

If I was really stressed out or lonely, I'd call Mom and Dad in the middle of the night.

(4 hours later in Fredericton.)

Sorry to wake you up, but she says she's not in love with me anymore!

I missed them horribly, but I knew I couldn't leave my life and go back to Fredericton. Things were different there...

Oy vey, Sarah! Not everything is a feminist battle! Relax!

Sweetie, I'm glad you're happy, but do you have to use the word "dyke"?

All I want is for some guy to ask me to marry him. Then my life will really start.

Signs

My mother had very firm principles, and she didn't mind telling you what they were.

I was often embarrassed by her zeal. She called my school in a rage after they used blackface in a play, lectured a waitress who used the term "Jewish lightning," and forbade me from having a friend over for dinner after I made the mistake of telling her that Oliver North was his hero.

She responded with this fierce, immediate love to people or animals who the rest of us avoided.

ugly nasty cat

crazy lady

bratty screaming child

She really never blended in.

Most People

After years of teaching young children, she got the perfect job: designing the kindergarten curriculum for the province of New Brunswick.

and supporting homeschooling parents.

Once that was done, she moved on to integrating kids with disabilities into regular classes...

She also spent hours worrying about corporal punishment, excessive testing, poor teaching, and cuts to the Department of Education.

Until, after 13 years, a new government came into power and laid off half the staff of the Department, including Mom.

For her, it was much more than losing a job. It was losing a battle against the forces of evil. She despaired for many months, until...

I'm going back to teaching kindergarten! I was never meant to be a bureaucrat anyway.

It didn't take Mom long to find a job. She came highly recommended.

...a competent, capable educator with a solid background in the theory of good elementary/early childhood education...

...a principal architect of the New Brunswick kindergarten curriculum heralded across Canada...

She has an excellent eye for detail, a tireless worker who gives generously of her time.

...Midge has worked to transform early childhood education in New Brunswick.

Without reservation, I give my endorsement...

Mom did great her first year back teaching. But the second year she changed schools and things didn't go so well. When the kids were bratty she couldn't control them.

It took her hours to clean up her classroom.

She was spending so long on lesson planning that she was working over 60 hours a week, even though she had co-written the provincial kindergarten curriculum.

Parents started to complain.

The principal brought in two young teachers to help her.

Hello, Mrs. Leavitt!

I wrote the kindergarten curriculum! Did you know that?

Over the Christmas holidays, she resigned.

Meanwhile, I was having problems of my own.

My girlfriend dumped me.

But I can't live without you!

I can't live without you either! But our love is killing me!

The feminist collective where I worked was imploding.

Mom? She broke up with me again and everyone at work hates me.

Mom and Dad came for a quick visit during this time. Something weird happened at the airport. When I came to meet them at the baggage carousel, Dad wasn't there. Mom didn't know where he had gone. A few minutes later he appeared; he said he'd told her he was going to the washroom.

Then at my apartment she couldn't get the sliding door to the bathroom open. She'd struggle with it until Dad or I came to help. She never got the hang of it.

The next time I called her to cry about my ex, she thought we were still together.

Hannah called and said that she thought Mom was acting weird too. She'd get confused about the strangest things, but if you tried to help her she got mad.

She's driving me crazy! She's just sad or angry all the time!

Mom told us everything was fine.

Maybe she was depressed about losing her job. Maybe it was menopause. Maybe she was having a midlife crisis or something. Maybe it would make more sense when I saw her in person again.

Arrival

Mom stayed in the background, all quiet. Usually she was the first to greet people, running out of the house as the car pulled up.

She was happy to see me.

But something was wrong.

The next morning when I came downstairs, Debbie and Dad were doing the New York Times crosswords that Debbie had photocopied and brought along. Hannah was in a bad mood and Sukey was trying to cheer her up. Mom was hovering.

Mom and I went for a walk.

I hadn't been back to Fredericton for three years, and I couldn't quite remember how to get to the river. Neither could Mom.

Eventually we got there. As we walked along, I wondered how to ask Mom what was wrong.

Look at the lovely flowers!

She'd stopped speaking to her friend because she'd asked what was wrong.

Sorry, Molly! I'll tell her you called.

And she was furious with Dad's sisters because Dad told her they'd asked too.

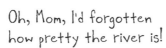

I decided not to say anything for now.

And see how they've replanted this garden area?

Oh, Mom, I'd forgotten how pretty the river is!

Isn't it just wonderful?

God I loved her hands.

She bit her nails and her veins stuck out all blue and lumpy. They weren't pretty hands. They were strong hands. Mom hands.

We all sat down. Dad didn't say anything, so I took a deep breath.

Um. We've noticed some stuff. Like you're really stressed out. Or sad. Um...

I have Alzheimer's.

 Did she know something? Was she up all night researching symptoms, trying to figure it all out, at the same time she was trying to pretend nothing was wrong?

Or was she just saying out loud the worst case scenario in order to ward it off?

Oy, Midge! You don't have Alzheimer's!

You know, Sarah, my own mother died so young. She never finished her life's work.

You don't know what's wrong, Mom. It's been a hard year. Talk to a counsellor or a doctor or something. Get some tests. You guys need help to figure this out.

They both sat and listened to me, like I knew something they didn't.

Then we ate dinner outside, as storm clouds gathered in the summer sky.

Thank you for talking to me, Sares. It was a gutsy thing to do.

That night I wrote a letter to Mom about making sure she asked for help when she needed it. I wrote a similar one to Dad.

In the morning Mom asked me to call Debbie to see if she could come back. Sukey had to go back to work but Debbie was off for the summer. She asked me to call Hannah too.

Debbie had barely unpacked but she said of course she'd come. Hannah started to cry and said she'd come too. She didn't seem angry anymore.

I left the next day. For the first time in many years it was difficult to say goodbye to my parents.

I spent the next eight hours worrying.

Donimo picked me up at the airport. It was good to see her. It was good to forget about Mom and Dad just a little bit.

As we headed to my place, I felt like I was running as fast as I could back to my own life, eager for relief.

Mom agreed to go to some appointments to try to figure out what was wrong.

ACKSON
IATRIST

The psychiatrist started out with some simple cognition tests that insulted her.

Please draw two clock hands on this clock face to represent two o'clock.

She told us that they were stupid, easy tests. But she couldn't do them.

They went to a naturopath next.

RATTLE RATTLE!

She told them that many things could cause Mom's symptoms.

Depression, vitamin deficiencies, heavy metal poisoning...

She encouraged them not to jump to conclusions. She gave Mom herbs and supplements and suggested she get some blood tests.

In the fall Dad would be on sabbatical from his job at the university. They had planned to spend the year in Mexico. They couldn't see any reason to cancel their plans.

Sunny Mexico

When we got off the plane in Oaxaca, the tarmac was boiling hot and the birds were singing.

We looked around for Mom and Dad.

Then we spotted them. Mom held her hands clenched in front of her like I'd noticed her doing in the summer.

At least she unclasped them long enough to hug me.

But her nails! They were long and red and fake.

In the cab, Mom picked her nails while Dad told us how one of his students had put them on for her, as a gift.

OAXACA TAXI

Mom didn't say anything.

We pulled up to their apartment.

It was surrounded by trees and flowers.

When Mom tried to get out of the cab, it was like she didn't understand the relationship between her foot and the ground.

I'm fine, Rob!

Honey, just put your foot all the way down!

Finally...

Come on, sweetie, let's get the girls some lunch.

There were orange trees all along the front of the apartment building. Mom started looking around on the grass underneath one of the trees.

Sarah? Look!

What, Mom?

See the hole in this orange? And it's hollow inside. The fruit bats come at night and suck out all the fruit.

What's wrong? I think it's so cute and smart of them!

Ugh!

In the evening, Donimo and I listened to the squeaks of the tiny bats in the orange tree. They seemed evil to me, killing the oranges, leaving them empty and dry.

eee! eee! eee!

Mom and Dad were surprised that we could hear the bats. They said they had not heard the high-pitched sounds.

The furniture in their place was massive, with rock-hard cushions. Dad said Oaxacan furniture was all like that.

It made me feel like a little kid.

Donimo and I slept on the couch and chair cushions on the living room floor. We had to whisper so Mom and Dad couldn't hear.

There's something wrong with her brain.

Yeah, I think you might be right.

Dad had to teach, so we went sightseeing with Mom. Dad told me and Donimo how to get to the big cemetery, Pantheon General.

Mom didn't remember how to get there, or never knew, or couldn't understand directions. It was hard to tell.

I have a photo of her smiling at the entrance to the catacombs.

She loved the way that Mexicans remembered and attended to their dead.

After a few days in the city, we drove to the coast in a tiny, borrowed car, along a narrow, winding road, dodging washouts and oncoming trucks.

HONK!

I got very carsick and had to lie down in the backseat. We drove for eight hours or so.

The landscape changed from dry scrub to jungle to pine forest. There were giant trees dripping with bromeliads and many signs that said "Curva Peligrosa."

huge plant that mezcal is made from

We arrived in Puerto Angel as night was falling. I had expected white sand, American tourists in bikinis. But Puerto Angel was a small fishing village, and the sand on the beach was brown, and instead of tourists there were fishing boats and local teenagers and dogs that seemed to belong to no one. The air smelled of smoke.

HOTEL Y RESTAURANT SORAYA

We stayed at the only hotel around, a large, yellow building on a rocky hill by the beach.

Mom got lost in the halls at the Soraya and we'd have to go looking for her.

She'd stand outside the car with her hand on the door handle, just stand there. If you told her to get in the car she got mad.

After a few days it was time to head back to the city. We'd come to love Puerto Angel and the coast and it was hard to leave.

This time I didn't get carsick. We stopped at an old lady's house in the jungle and ate homemade chorizo.

In the afternoon we left the mountains. Dad started speeding. Then Donimo yelled.

ROB!

A dead dog lay in the middle of the road. Another dog was sniffing it.

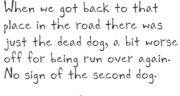

THUNK!

Dad kept right on driving...

and driving, like he was in a daze.

Donimo started to cry. Mom didn't do anything. She just kept staring out the window.

Dad! Are you going to turn around or anything?

What for?

What's wrong with you, Dad? That dog could be suffering!

Jesus Christ, OK!

skreech!

When we got back to that place in the road there was just the dead dog, a bit worse off for being run over again. No sign of the second dog.

Dad and I got out of the car and spotted the dog under a bush, snarling.

Then it ran away at full speed.

It's fine. Let's go.

Poor thing. We should see if someone owns it.

No se. Tal vez mi vecino, pero...

Gracias!

The dog ran off, Donimo. It must be OK.

No, it's probably in shock.

My mom, animal lover, didn't say a word. And Dad just kept sighing.

That poor fucking dog. We hit it so hard.

Yeah. I guess Dad is just really preoccupied.

Sarah, can you believe Mom didn't even notice when we hit that dog?

You seem so far away, Mom. What's wrong?

Maybe I'm just thinking about things that have nothing to do with you!

Waiting

When Mom and Dad came back from Mexico, they stayed with family in the States before returning to New Brunswick. Dad's father took him aside. "You can't wait anymore," he said. "You have to take Midge to a neurologist." Dad started to protest. "It doesn't matter if she gets mad," Grandpa said. "You have to do something!" So Dad talked to Mom. She did get mad. But she agreed to go to the neurologist.

I made the appointment for when you guys are here, so you can come with us.

That's great, Dad.

They had both changed in the few months since we'd last seen them. Dad looked older. Mom looked even more out of it. She was wearing a puffy hat with multicoloured stripes.

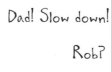

SOB! Mom!

Oh sweetie, I love you!

Well, let's get the luggage into the car.

Here, Rob, have one of these chocolates I brought from Vancouver.

Great chocolates!

Dad! Slow down!

Rob?

My chocolates!

Dad! You ate all of Donimo's chocolates!

Shh! Don't worry, Rob, I don't mind.

Did you see Mom's new hat? It's from one of the Guatemalan students.

MOW!

Rob? Can I help?

Dad! Don't take all the heavy stuff! You'll hurt your back!

I'm fine.

MEOW!

Oh Kitty! Hello!

Come on, Midge!

MRROW!

Dad put Donimo and me in the attic bedroom, where they kept Hannah's and my old books and toys. A collection of rubber animals whose heads kept falling off. The dollhouse they had built for us and wired with electric lights.

Mom had made a tiny Leavitt family to go with the house. She made the Sarah doll younger than the Hannah doll, to try to help us understand our relationship to each other — big sister, little sister — through imaginative play.

Dad had hung a painting on the wall that he bought in Oaxaca of a man with his heart being torn out by a demon woman. The air in the attic was hot and dusty.

MMMPH

The next morning I ran downstairs as soon as I woke up.

Good morning, Mom. What are you doing?

Oh, just trying to keep track of my blankety-blank headaches.

Can I see?

Sure. It's not very interesting.

She was writing in a tiny journal with a purple cover that had two flies on it.

Headaches — MSL
June 9, 99
starting

Inside there were tiny notes...

OK. So. Midge Leavitt.

Let's see here.

What day is it today, Midge?

WHAT YEAR IS IT?

WHERE DO YOU WORK?

WHERE DO YOU LIVE?

HOW OLD ARE YOU?

WHAT DID YOU EAT FOR BREAKFAST?

Hmm.

I wanted to ask you about these headaches I've been having.

So Robert, has Midge exhibited any inappropriate behaviour?

CONFUSION?

MOOD

SWINGS?

OUTBURSTS?

Well, not... I guess it just seems that she's having trouble with a lot of daily tasks. Right honey?

CAN SHE DRESS HERSELF?

DRIVE?

FEED HERSELF?

BATHE?

CLEAN?

READ?

Language

Mom started at Radcliffe College in 1962. She was very cool.

She wore a genuine peacoat and she smoked.

She met Dad, a Harvard student, in their final year. They always laughed about how well-behaved and naive they both were.

They each got drunk once in college. Mom spent an evening on top of a refrigerator.

Dad walked across Harvard Yard barefoot in the winter.

A few months after they started dating, Dad gave Mom an engagement ring he'd made himself, a copper band that turned her finger green.

They had a small wedding. Dad's sisters cried to see him go, and Mom always held it against them.

They had two kids and moved to the country...

where they built a life of books and art and creativity. They never owned a television.

Hannah and I grew up surrounded by beloved characters from our favourite books, from Oz, Narnia, Middle Earth, Moominland.

TIK-TOK OF OZ

Many of them seemed like our intimate friends.

SNUFKIN

We all loved The Lord of the Rings. The Black Riders terrified us.

Dad and I cried together when Gandalf died.

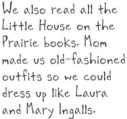

We also read all the Little House on the Prairie books. Mom made us old-fashioned outfits so we could dress up like Laura and Mary Ingalls.

Mom and Dad must have read to us almost every day of our childhoods.

They also loved making up nicknames for us, especially Dad. I was Sarah Beanstalk for Sarah Beatrice, and Large Brown Woman for some unknown reason.

Hannah was Hanner, because that's how they said it in Maine, and 14 Women for no reason, and Wim because it was short for 14 Women.

Dad was RML, his initials, and Mom was many things, including Migdel, a variation of Midge, which then became Mrs. Migdelpopper.

Our first cat, Emily, was Beelzebub or Beels or Kitten Kaboodle.

In junior high, Hannah took our language play to the next level with a collection of acronyms and made-up words that were so apt that Dad and Mom and I adopted many of them for our own use. Like if a couple was having an overly affectionate goodbye, we'd say they were being "piss," short for "parting is such sweet sorrow."

No one in our family was good at sports.

Strike 5! OK, everyone, let's give Sarah a few more chances to hit the ball!

What? That's not fair!

We're gonna be here forever!

But we were great spellers.

Come on, Mom, ask me another one! Make it harder this time!

And we learned to play cutthroat Scrabble at a very young age.

We were never forbidden to swear, but Mom sent us out to the treehouse

when we got too preoccupied with bodily functions.

The forbidden words were insults or anything racist. Then you risked getting your mouth washed out with soap.

If you didn't know what a word meant or how to spell it, you looked it up. We did this all the time, just for fun.

The Oxford English Dictionary had such tiny letters that it came with a magnifying glass in a little drawer.

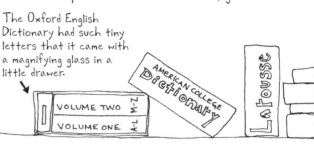

Dad liked to draw weird little creatures and write mysterious poems that fascinated and infuriated me and Hannah because we didn't understand them. Mom wrote and drew all the time. When I was away at university, she used to send me notes and doodles from the endless work meetings that drove her crazy. She loved words and hated how the bureaucrats she worked for made up jargon or misused words in an effort to sound smart.

Mom and Dad were both teachers and teachers of teachers, and they relied on each other for advice and editing.

You're absolutely right!

Rob, I think if you switch these paragraphs around, it will be a lot clearer.

They were always ranting about the school system.

If the lessons are boring and simplistic, why would the students feel motivated?

Exactly. They need a challenge.

"The gifted teacher is the one who helps develop children's eagerness to look and touch into a hunger to understand. Children motivated from within have a powerful capacity to concentrate, persevere, and succeed."
– Midge Leavitt

Our parents taught us, as very young children, that language, words, and books belonged to us, that they were exciting and powerful, and that being smart and good with words was one of the most important things to strive for.

I made up my own language!

I taught children to love reading!

I wrote a weird poem!

I beat Dad at Scrabble!

Diagnosis

That fall while we waited for the test results, Mom wrote to me a few times on index cards in marker. One letter included curling red maple leaves wrapped in a napkin.

Thought you'd like some damn colours for your birth. Extras enclosed for Donamo.

I asked her to write down some things about my childhood, since her long-term memory was still good and mine never had been. She was excited about writing a lot of lists for me, but she only managed one.

Do Do you remember when Emily Dour Foxcroft was lost and do you remember when she came back.

Do you remember when I helped you and Debby Grant make taper your blue jean legs

Do you remember making neat little catalogues of make-up and clothing

And do you remember spending lots of time playing with the doll house and dolls

It took me a while to decipher her new handwriting.

There is no blood test or anything that can definitively diagnose someone with Alzheimer's disease. A neurologist observes the patient's behaviour and symptoms, and carries out a series of tests to rule out other possibilities and make a probable diagnosis.

The only way to prove it was Alzheimer's was to do a brain biopsy, which was very painful, or to wait until an autopsy could be performed.

Dad's cousin and Mom's cousin were both respected neurologists in the States. The doctor in Fredericton consulted with them. Mom and Dad drove down to the Lahey Clinic where Dad's cousin worked. They did more cognitive tests. They considered all possible diagnoses.

case
research
guess
could
be
test
rare
infection
few
biopsy
chance
doubt
test
test
deficiency
hope
small possibility
maybe
eliminate
percentage
indications

Mom had an MRI, a CAT scan, and a PET scan. She didn't have a brain tumour or a blood clot or any signs of stroke.

There were no clear signs of the brain atrophy caused by Alzheimer's, but it could just be too soon to tell.

She had a spinal tap, which ruled out some rare diseases of the central nervous system caused by tuberculosis and syphilis.

She had blood tests and urine tests for diabetes and infections and other conditions and deficiencies.

The tests all came back negative. Dad's cousin said there was a chance that Mom could have a rare neurological disease that caused similar symptoms. But it was a miniscule chance and you could only tell for sure with a brain biopsy and the treatment was extremely painful and not guaranteed to work. Mom decided not to have the biopsy.

On October 6, 1999, Mom and Dad met with their neurologist. He said that all other possibilities had now been ruled out and the test results pointed to Alzheimer's. There was nothing else to try. Dad told me that as they left the clinic, he said to Mom, "It's not how we planned things, is it, Midge?"

He can't remember whether or not she answered him.

I hate what's happening to me.

Part Two

Please

When I was growing up, I was a little bit confused about God and religion. We were Jewish, but my parents were not religious, and we never were part of any Jewish community. I remember asking Mom and Dad more than once whether or not they believed in God.

Oy vey, I'm not sure. I think so.

Of course I don't! If there was a God, the world wouldn't be in such a mess!

But sometimes Mom changed her tune.

Of course you fell and hurt yourself! That's God punishing you for hitting your sister!

WAHH!

Mom loved teaching us about our Jewish heritage.

Your great-great-aunt Manya escaped from Russia...

We celebrated Hanukkah, and Mom said the prayers even when Dad had to help her with the words.

Baruch atoy... um...

The only other holiday we celebrated was Passover. I think mostly because Mom loved the songs and the theme of liberation.

She liked pointing out the Jewish-sounding lyrics when we listened to reggae.

Zion train is comin our way!

She got very angry at me when I went through a period of telling other kids I wasn't Jewish.

I remember her being upset about Malcolm Ross, a New Brunswick teacher who denied the Holocaust.

At the same time, she couldn't stand the Fredericton Jewish community, which was mostly wealthy and conservative.

She wouldn't ever have gone to a synagogue to find solace, which is what I did when she got sick.

I had never been to a synagogue before. This one was Renewal. While many of the practices were very traditional...

women participated equally.

And newcomers were welcomed, even if, like me, they had no idea what was going on.

After I had gone to services a few times, I went to see the rabbi.

RABBI'S OFFICE

I told him about my mother and he listened for a long time.

Then he taught me the prayer for healing: El na refah na la. It means, "Heal her, please."

It's what Moses said to God when Miriam was struck with leprosy. I liked the sound of the words and I liked that they were first spoken for someone named Miriam, which was my mother's name.

I liked the prayer even though there was no chance of my mother ever being healed.

I put the prayer beside her photo like a charm.

The Most Important

One time Mom was trying to tell us something.

She got very upset because she couldn't remember the name of the person she was talking about.

She kept repeating, "He was the most important!"

Dad kept trying to guess who it was, and finally he asked her if she was talking about Abraham Lincoln. "Yes!" she said, and started to cry.

Then she said to Dad, "That's right, right?"

"That people shouldn't have slaves?"

"Yes."

"Yes, sweetie. Of course that's right."

Learning to Laugh

When Mom and Dad visited me in Vancouver, I used to send them off sightseeing while I stayed home and gossiped on the phone or went out with my friends.

The Christmas after the diagnosis, my parents came to visit me. I regretted ever being so wasteful of the time I had with them. This visit I made sure I would be available to them for the whole week.

I sublet a suite for them in the house where I lived.

It was a small suite on the top floor with a shared bathroom. I warned the other tenants that my mother had Alzheimer's so she might act weird sometimes.

That's so sad!

When they arrived and we were all in the same house, I felt better for some reason. Like we were safer from the disease when we were together.

But it wasn't true. Mom went to pat the cat and didn't seem to notice when he moved.

We went to visit a friend of mine. Mom remembered her and was thrilled to see her.

Then she kept pointing at a photo on the fridge and asking the same questions about it over and over.

We went to see a Cuban band.

We all dressed up. Dad asked Mom to dance in this really sweet formal way.

Madame?

On the dance floor, Mom froze.

She seemed confused and scared.

Dad led her in tiny circles.

The next morning I watched out the window as he walked away across the park.

I went upstairs to see Mom.

Hi honey! I'm going to get in the shower.

She walked out into the hall with no pants on.

I waited for her and thought about how they used to dance so freely and joyfully that I'd get embarrassed.

Dad came back with coffee from his favourite Italian café.

What's it like, Dad?

I don't know. I guess sometimes it turns out that everything you thought about how the future would be just isn't true.

After they left my friend came to see me.

God, your Mom is fucking hilarious! She just kept saying the same thing over and over and over! Ha ha!

Ha ha ha ha ha ha

What's wrong, Sarah? You know, the only way you're going to get through this is if you relax and learn to laugh about it!

Garlic chive seeds from
Mom's and Dad's garden.
May they flourish in
              Vancouver

♥
from
Mom + Dad to Sarah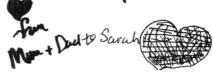

Shadowing

The next summer, Dad went back to Oaxaca for six weeks to visit and teach. He needed a break from Mom.

He had arranged with me and Debbie to stay with Mom while he was gone. We tried to act like we were coming to visit her, not to take care of her.

Debbie said she'd go for the first month.

I said I'd go for the last two weeks.

Hannah said she would visit, but she would not stay alone with Mom.

I'm just not like you and Debbie, OK? I'm not strong like you guys.

When I arrived some friends gave me a ride from the airport. It was almost midnight but the air was still thick and hot. I felt sick wondering what Mom would be like.

Midgie! Sarah's here! This way!

Hannah and Debbie gave me gifts for my 31st birthday, which had just passed. There was nothing from Mom and Dad. I tried not to pout. Mom and Dad had always showered us with gifts.

Mom had made me a card.

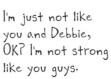

P.S. please help us to find you a vase for you and your flowers when they bloom

Debbie was doing her usual big sister bossy thing with Mom. I could see that Hannah was sick of it already. Mom didn't seem too happy either.

Debbie started updating me about distant relatives I had never met.

Hannah filled me in on her boyfriend and which girls were after him.

Mom just sat there.

49

This is the story, without all the pauses:

I went to Pam Wong's house to get my legs waxed. Robert drove me there but I decided to walk home afterwards.

I knew I had to walk down Smythe Street to our house. Part way down, I got lost. I mean, I could see where I had to go, but I couldn't figure out how to get there. It seemed so far away.

I ended up outside Harvey's, where you used to go, remember? I could see further down the hill, but it didn't make sense. Then a lovely young woman came along.

Are you OK?

No. I'm trying to get home and I can't.

Maybe someone at Harvey's can help you get a cab.

So I went inside. A nice young man was mopping the floor.

Your feet hurt?

No, my feet are fine. I'm lost.

He called me a cab and I told the driver what happened.

I got lost. Because I have Alzheimer's.

Alzheimer's. Phew. That's rough. My dad had it, used to go out to the bar in the middle of the night.

People here are so kind. They really care. I'm so lucky.

This is my new bracelet. It's from the police in case I get lost. But I'll never go out again by myself.

Food

When Hannah and I were growing up, Mom did her best to feed us healthy food. Like soup made from vegetables she'd grown from seed, and homemade bread.

Yuck!

I hate this!

After we moved out and had to fend for ourselves, we appreciated it more.

Welcome home, sweetie! I made some salad from the garden and muffins and...

Let's eat!

When Mom got sick, everything changed.

First the garden. Dad took on the planning and the soil preparation. He bought the seeds. Mom helped with weeding and harvesting.

But she couldn't manage to squat or kneel.

Even when she only meant to pull weeds, she pulled up lots of other plants too.

And she couldn't cook.

Tools became weapons.

Things got ruined.

Sometimes we'd give her a carrot and a dull knife and let her "help."

I miss... ten-pound loaves of dark rye, dense stews of vegetables grown from seed, with tofu mixed in to make it "proteinacious," a.k.a. "good 'n' good for you," honey carob cookies, homemade yoghurt...

rumble! growl!

Imagine, in the grief and silence of that house, Dad trying to cook for Mom.

Can I help, Rob?

No, it's OK.

Not that he couldn't cook. Far from it. Dad loved cooking as much as Mom did, though he was more likely to make treats.

← popovers for Sunday brunch

But when Mom got sick, he started making a lot of pasta with sauce from a jar.

Oh lovely! Thank you!

SPLAT

Or they just didn't eat. Mom often didn't feel hunger (one of the effects of Alzheimer's), and Dad was probably just too depressed.

As Mom got sicker and their meals got smaller, I turned into some sort of...

extreme Jewish mother, obsessed with making them eat.

That summer it got really bad. One morning I came downstairs to the kitchen. Debbie was burning eggs in blackened oil.

Look! I made Midgie some lovely breakfast!

No thank you!

The kitchen was like a billboard with huge letters saying, ALZHEIMER'S LIVES HERE! YOUR MOTHER IS GONE.

Um, no thank you, Deb. I don't like eggs.

Something had to be done.

I took Mom's vegetarian cookbooks upstairs and made a shopping list.

I went to Superstore and burned through the aisles.

ESS! ESS!

When I got home, they were all still in the kitchen.

Hi Sarah! Can you think of a city in northern Italy that has 7 letters in its name? Starts with T.

Can I help?

I'm starving. What did you get me?

I hated them all and I didn't ask for any help.

Over the next week, I got into a routine.

Sorting through her drawers for dirty clothes that she'd put away.

socks | undies
shirts
sweaters

Drying her back.

Tucking her in. It wasn't so bad.

Some things became precious to me, like her poetic mistakes.

Doesn't the grass feel lovely and green today?

And the times she read aloud from old favourites. When she missed words or even whole paragraphs you knew that soon she wouldn't be reading at all.

I got less scared of being alone with Mom. And I got more annoyed with Debbie.

It's really dusty under my chair.

Yup.

When Mom couldn't think of a word, Debbie would jump in and finish her sentence.

and uh, the uh, uh...

the kitty came home!

If Mom was being especially unreasonable, Debbie would roll her eyes at me like we were in it together.

For the first time in my life, Mom complained to me about her big sister.

What's wrong with Debbie? Why does she act like that?

You could ask her, Mom.

No.

So I took matters into my own hands.

Remember you said you'd understand if I wanted alone time with Mom?

Well yes, but.

A few days later, the three of us went to visit some friends in Maine. Then Debbie headed back to New York and Mom and I drove home, just the two of us.

As we turned onto the highway, I put in the Buena Vista Social Club CD. Mom's face lit up and she turned to me.

De Alto Cedro voy para Macané
Luego a Cueto voy para Mayarí

Oh! Doesn't this music just reach right in and grab your heart?

Psycho Killer

The Alzheimer's Society materials said it was important to talk about the future.

But we were all so scared and silent.

In the first years of her illness, it often seemed like Mom didn't understand that her condition was terminal.

The Aricept is helping me, right Rob?

Please can we call the neurologist right now and ask her if I'll get better?

At other times she just denied that there was anything wrong at all.

Leave me alone! I don't need babysitting!

All the brochures said you should talk to patients while they could still understand and express their wishes. One morning Mom was having her usual breakfast: Toast with almond butter and grapefruit sections.

I started crying, but I was careful not to make any noise.

Then I just couldn't be quiet anymore.

Mom?

Yes sweetie?

I'm really glad we're spending so much time together.

Me too.

I'm trying to spend as much time with you as I can.

That's great, darling.

Because you're sick.

I want to see you as much as I can before...

before you die.

Mom?

Everybody dies.

But if you have Alzheimer's you die sooner.

Taste and Smell

One of the first things that happened to Mom when she got sick was that she lost her sense of smell. This can be a sign of Alzheimer's. But that was before we even suspected that she had something serious. She just couldn't smell.

Of course later we realized: it was one of the first steps in her separation from the world.

It frightened her.

She could not smell garlic or apples or tomatoes that had warmed in the summer sun.

 Mom had never let us have sugar when we were kids.

And she never craved it herself. Unlike me. I gorged on it in secret.

But as her sense of smell diminished, she seemed to discover the pleasure of sweetness on the tongue.

She began to grab at sugar.

She ate as much as she could, even when she couldn't figure out how to unwrap it.

Mom forgot more and more of herself.

She didn't know that she thought sugar was evil. She only knew it tasted good. I used to hide candy so I wouldn't get in trouble. Now I hid it so she wouldn't eat it all.

Mom dressed herself in odd collections of garments from different seasons and occasions.

Guatemalan hat almost always
messy hair
accessories and footwear carried around until abandoned
turtleneck even when hot
dressy office skirt
socks • undies • shirts • sweaters

Sometimes she realized what she was doing partway through. Maybe I could start a new style!

Mom wore winter clothes that summer, so she sweated a lot.

And she didn't brush her teeth very well, so her breath stank.

I was so embarrassed. It reminded me of when I was a teenager and I wouldn't walk with her at the mall because she dressed weird.

Me: Bathroom stuff seems harder for you lately.

Mom: Oy.

Me: Yeah...

Mom: Harder... that's not fair is it?

Me: No, none of it's fair at all, Mom.

Trouble Understanding

Most people in my family have curly hair. It was one of the things that made us really stand out in the small towns we lived in when I was growing up.

Mom had tried to straighten her hair for a while in the 60s. She ironed it.

She rolled it tightly around large juice cans.

ow.

She and Dad both tried a thick, waxy product meant for black people's hair. It stuck in their hair for months.

In the late 70s, Mom got her hair cut in a short, round afro-ish style. When she came home, I told her she looked "perfectly hideous." I like to think I was just trying out new vocabulary.

From about the mid 80s on, Mom wore her hair the same way: long, pulled back in a ponytail, usually a little fuzzy.

My friends' moms had tight perms. They also wore a lot of makeup.

I saw your mother the other day, Sarah. I could tell it was her, even from the back. No one else wears their hair like that! Bless her heart.

When I was little, Mom had to fight with me to brush the knots out of my hair. She wrote me a story with pictures about me running away to escape the hairbrush. It was called Sarah and the Monster. In the story I hide in a tunnel and meet a monster.

The monster goes and takes my place at home because she actually wants her hair brushed.

After a few weeks or months I give up and come out of the tunnel. When Mom sees me, we run towards each other so fast that there is a huge bump when we meet. We kiss and hug and jump up and down and twirl around and around.

Then I let her brush my hair and only scream and bite a little bit because I am so glad to be home again with my mom.

This is the kind of thing I would think about whenever I washed or untangled my mom's hair when she was sick.

I never used a comb or brush on Mom's hair, just my fingers. At some point I started putting little balls of her hair in my pocket instead of throwing them away.

And then I started collecting my own hair. Every time I washed my hair or ran my fingers through it, I kept the loose hairs. It did not take long to collect boxes of dense, springy clumps of hair.

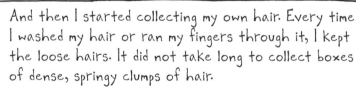

January - Sept 2000

Some of my friends found it disturbing.

Eek!

I found it comforting. I collected more and more and more.

Sept 01 - Mar 02

April - Aug. 2001

I kept the boxes on shelves above the bed and it helped me sleep at night, just knowing they were there.

A Small Joke

We were listening to Bob Marley, but I can't remember
which song. Probably One Foundation or Positive Vibration.

Did he say constipation?
Oh, excuse me!

Kitty, The

My parents used to have a cat that everyone called The Kitty. She was even addressed that way, as in "Hello, The Kitty," or "Come here, The Kitty."

Mom had named her Lucy when they first got her, and it pissed her off when we called her The Kitty. But we couldn't help it.

The summer that Mom started getting sick, The Kitty stopped eating and drinking.

The vet came to the house and put her to sleep while Mom held her.

Ready, Midge?

They buried her in the garden and planted a miniature rosebush on her grave.

They spent a year in mourning.

The next summer they got another black cat from the SPCA. We all had trouble remembering the former cat; the two blended together into one continuous female black cat.

Mom named this one Lucy, too, and we tried harder this time to call her by that name.

But it was still a challenge.

Hi The Kit... I mean, Lucy.

Lucy was stocky, with small ears and round, close-set eyes.

She looked like the offspring of the Owl and the Pussycat.

Mom loved all animals. But she was obsessed with Lucy.

There you are, darling!

Oh! Look how smart she is!

Beautiful!

Just look at her eating her food!

Lucy never seemed to care about people that much.

She spent a good part of the day under the covers on Mom and Dad's bed.

Or under the shed.

Or in the tall grass near the garden.

According to Mom, Lucy was very affectionate.

But not long after they got Lucy, Mom's movements got too unpredictable for any cat, especially an aloof one.

Lucy! Come here, darling, so I can brush you!

Lucy only cuddled with Dad. She sat on his lap occasionally, and he would rest his coffee cup on her flat head. She seemed to like it.

After a brief period of sleeping on my parents' bed at night, Lucy didn't come near Mom much at all. But Mom never seemed to realize this.

She would always ask where Lucy was when she went to bed. At some point we started lying and saying that Lucy was in the room. It helped her calm down and go to sleep.

Sometimes Mom's undying love for Lucy drove me crazy. It pissed me off that she couldn't see what Lucy was really like.

Kitty KITTY KITTY kitty! Kitty kitty KITTY KITTY kitty Kitty

Lucy! You don't know how good you have it here, ungrateful cat!

I sometimes got a small, mean satisfaction from speaking the unspeakable.

She's the coldest cat I've ever met!

Shh! Huh?

But then I would relent.

Wow, Mom, look how great Lucy is!

Yeah!

I made Mom little books about Lucy, and cards and small photo albums. She liked to carry them around.

Queen Lucy by Sarah

Happy Mother's Day!

PHOTOS of KITTY for MOM

She recognized and talked about Lucy even when she seemed confused about who I was.

Is it weird to be jealous of a cat?

One Sunday morning a close friend of mine called to tell me that her grandmother had killed herself.

I had met her once. She was a wealthy, elegant old lady.

They found her in her car in the closed carport with the engine running.

She had left a medical book on her coffee table.

It was open to the chapter on Alzheimer's.

The same day I heard about this, Mom and Dad called for our usual Sunday chat.

When I asked Mom how she was, she told Dad to go outside so she could talk to me privately.

I don't want to be married anymore!

Shit. Mom had never talked to me about marriage problems or anything like that. I was her kid, not her confidante.

I'M a NOBODY!

I'm not a REAL PERSON anymore!

Then she started crying really hard. I decided to pretend she wasn't my mother so I could manage to stay on the phone and listen to her.

Mmm hmm. Oh it must be so hard.

Yes I'm sure you do.

And how do you feel about that?

She said Dad was treating her like a child. She wanted to live by herself. She wanted to be left alone. We talked for an hour or so. Then...

OK. So you're going to sit down with Dad and tell him how you feel? Promise? Great.

Click.

WAAAH! I want my MOMMY!

The next day Dad called.

How is everything with Mom?

Mew!

Well she came downstairs this morning and said, "Sarah says we need to talk."

She told me how pissed off she was about lots of things.

I guess it needed to be said.

But I really can't stop doing things like picking up after her.

Or reminding her to do stuff.

Maybe I could be nicer.

Shut up, Dad! You're great with her!

She asked me how long she'd had this disease.

Then she said, "How much longer till I can die?"

What did you say?

I said something about hoping they'd find a cure.

She said she used to have hope but not anymore.

I think she wants to kill herself but she isn't capable of it now.

Hello? Sarah?

Love to Donimo

Hope you like Bmbws.
See you soon
family is The whole
eags to see you
from Midge

Gaps

I spent the next summer writing left-handed to strengthen my brain. I filled pages and pages with alphabets and encouraging notes to myself.

ABCDEFGHIJKLMNOPQRSTUVWXYZ
abcdefghijklmnopqrstuvwxyz saran

getting better!

When I visited Mom, I wrote left-handed every night in one journal and kept my sketches and notes in another.

She points to things— sometimes in the wrong direction or at the wrong thing. She wiggles her index finger at things or at you when she can't think of the right word and she wants you to know what she means...

She wiggles her finger, then sees her finger wiggling and wiggles the finger on her other hand, then rubs that finger all over her other hand. Why?

Mom did not know what "tank top" meant.

She didn't recognize pineapple weed, which we always called chamomile, and which we used to pick and eat together when I was a kid.

matricaria discoidea

One day we took a walk and we passed a preteen boy on the street.

Oh! That was Jessica. How nice of her to remember us!

One morning she stood behind me grinding her teeth as I tried to eat some eggs.

CRUNCH! CRUNCH!

I have good news for you and Hannah. Things are getting better. Lots of research.

I knew what she meant. Research for a cure for Alzheimer's. I lost my appetite.

One day we were all sitting around talking about not remembering books or movies and watching them again and realizing we'd already seen them. Mom said ruefully, "Every day is like that for me. I get up and I think it's a new early morning and Rob says no, it's 11 PM."

Bird Brain

I couldn't do the work I'd brought with me to Fredericton.

Tweet!
Too-weet!
Twee!
Twee!
Twee!

Mom wouldn't stop making these weird noises.

Mom!

Tuh-woo!
Tuwit,
Tuwoo!
Twoo!

Until all of a sudden she got very quiet.

Mom?

Mom?

I found her on the sun porch, pointing out the window and wiggling her finger.

She liked to stand there and watch the birds at the feeder.

Aren't they just so, so...

So what, Mom?

Twee!

Aren't they just so what?

She was pointing at the birds, but they'd flown away already. I knew that but I pretended to have no idea what she was trying to say. I was sick of trying to fill in the gaps in her speech. I was sick of helping her. I was sick of her being sick.

She stared at me, her smile gone, her finger not wiggling anymore.

Later, when the anger had evaporated, I was filled with guilt and then fear. I had a vision of myself as a child, trying to grasp her leg as she fluttered away to join the birds. I couldn't hold her here on earth with me, no matter how hard I tried.

I Wasn't There

There was still lots to be done.

Look at my ring!

Drawing a picture of the bride and groom on the cover of the guest book...

Guest Book

Packaging the favours...

Meanwhile there was Mom, a little worse than the last visit. The doors were all locked because she'd wandered away a few times.

Copying the program...

Program
the marriage of Hannah & Jordan

The last dress fitting...

Choosing Mom's wedding outfit.

The day finally came.

I felt like I needed to stay at Hannah's side.

She missed Mom so much, even though she was still alive.

No one could take Mom's place.

Though I couldn't help thinking...

Mom might not have been very supportive.

She'd never approved of religion.

Least of all Orthodox Judaism.

Most rabbis in New Brunswick were Orthodox, so my sister, who'd never embraced her Jewishness until she got a Jewish boyfriend, was now having an Orthodox wedding. This meant that only Dad was involved in the ceremony and all he did was walk her down the aisle.

In spite of all my misgivings, it was impossible not to cry. Hannah looked so beautiful and Dad looked so proud. I tried to get Mom to turn around but she wouldn't.

At the reception we danced.

Dad got tipsy and tried to get Mom to sit on his lap but her body wouldn't bend. Debbie and Sukey took her home.

A few days later I showed Mom some photos from the wedding.

It was fun, wasn't it, Mom?

I don't know. I wasn't there!

Water

I choked on some food and started drinking water from my glass.

Mom: Are you OK? Why don't you have some water?

Me: I am, I'm drinking water right now.

Mom: I mean for your coughing.

Mom: Ooh, I would love lots and lots of water.

[Drinks three small glasses.]

See how happy she was with all that water?

Finally

Thunderstorm

Mom started running ahead of us.
She looked so normal when she ran.
For some reason she looked more
coordinated.

Run Away!

SHUFFLE
SHUFFLE

Mom came out of the bathroom
and started wandering off down
the hall. "I feel left out," she
murmured to herself.

How's it going, Mom?

Oh, I think it's going
quite sadly.

Part Three

Things that Mom liked to carry around

Mom liked to carry things with her when she wandered around the house.
She'd go through phases of carrying the same thing for a while.

> cat brush
> weeds from the garden
> photos of her parents
> greeting cards
> books I made her
> socks
> The Lord of the Rings, Book One: The Fellowship of the Ring
> napkins
> bits of houseplants

Dec 21, 2001
Waiting for Mom to finish in the bathroom, so I'm just writing for a while...

Like I ever wanted to be so familiar with her body, her bad breath, her smelly underarms,

her skinny body huddling in the bath as she looks up at me wide-eyed.

Like this?

Like this?

She means, "Do I get out of the tub like this?"

Hmm?

It gets hard to see someone as a person when they've become a list of needs: BATH, CLOTHES, BRUSH TEETH, WALK, FOOD, ETC.

If you just think about that list, then you're not as sad... until one night you're giving her pills and she starts pretending to be a monster...

Gobbledy Gobbledy! Hee hee!

And she's a person again and you don't only love her, you like her.

If only I could just stay mad or annoyed or neutral. Is Mom done yet? Better go see.

Here Mom, let me help you up.

That year there was a song on the radio called Last Resort by Papa Roach. It ran through my head a lot of the time, like a soundtrack to her struggling.

Cut my life into pieces

This is my last resort

Suffocation, No breathing,

Don't give a fuck if I cut my arm bleeding

Donimo and I were staying with Mom while Dad visited our family in the States. I left Donimo in our usual bed in the attic and slept in my old bedroom, across the hall from Mom, so I could hear her as soon as she got up in the morning.

One morning I heard her rummaging around in her room but I didn't feel like getting up yet.

Then she came into my room.

Phew!

I pretended to be asleep, like I used to do when I was a kid.

Phew!

When I finally gave up and opened my eyes, she just stared at me until I spoke.

Hi Mom.

Then she turned around and left.

She called to me from her room.

Sarah! Do you want to look?

Look at what?

Look at what, Mom?

I just think it's so.

It's so what?

It had snowed during the night and everything outside was glittering.

Look!

One night after that, Donimo and I were watching TV.

I'm going upstairs to pee. Let me know what I miss.

Sniff! Sob!

Mom? Can I come in?

Yeah.

Questions

Mom: Are you guys guy?
So you don't have to
wonder about.

Me: Are you comfortable, Mom?
Mom: I don't know.

Mom: Am I a stringle?

Me: Are you OK, Mom?
Mom: No. I just can't tell what is and isn't.

Mom: Honey, can I open
your voice?

Me: Oh, Mom, I thought you were sleeping.
Mom: I don't know if I am or not.

I decided to take a couple of creative writing classes to help me write about what was happening to our family. I told Mom and Dad what I was doing.

It helps to get it down on paper. I really want to record this.

That's great, sweetie.

Yeah.

You can read it to us when you come.

Pardon?

So when I got there in the summer...

Are you sure you want to hear this?

Yes.

Mom, you know this is about you being sick, right?

Oh! What a good thing to write about.

OK. I hope you like it.

Uh. This is about the, uh, first summer.

After I'd read a page or two, Mom tried to stand up and slid off the couch and onto the floor. She started to cry.

OH!

This is a hard thing to say.

I'm not a real person.

You all. It makes me.

Do you like me?

The scariest thing is the things I don't know.

I didn't try that again.

Y Tu Loquita

I think the kitty can
see what I'm thinking.
I really do.

Outsiders

Of course there's no way Dad could have taken care of Mom without hired help. For most of Mom's illness, Kim and Joanne* were there when Dad was at work or sometimes if he just needed to get out. I always thought about how normal these two women were in the outside world, and how alien they were to our family.

Dad hired Kim first, when he finally admitted that Mom couldn't stay alone. He told Mom that Kim was just there to clean.

Joanne started when Mom needed even more help.

Kim was always saying things that seemed inappropriate, in her thick New Brunswick accent.

Look, Midgie! Yer boyfriend's home! Let's not tell him about our wild partyin, eh?

She was a quiet, gentle woman, trained to do personal care.

Hello, Robert. She's been sleeping for a while now. Dinner's all ready to go.

Mom got mad at both of them, especially when she was still well enough to know that they were there to take care of her.

We can't come meet you at the doctor's, Robert. She won't get in the car.

Well, she's sure a barrel of laughs today. Won't even get dressed.

Cooking for Mom was challenging for Kim and Joanne. Mom was vegetarian, plus I kept sending Dad notes about weird healthy things to add to her food, since she didn't eat very much.

True to form, Mom came to like the abrasive Kim, partly because Kim had a young daughter and loved to get ideas from Mom about children's books.

We all loved Joanne, who definitely found our family weird, but seemed to like us more for it.

So I guess you'd be Midge's daughter-in-law, Donimo!

Oh you two are so sweet!

And how are you today, Mrs. Migdel?

Kim and Joanne usually got a break when I visited. I'd take over the cooking and feeding and bathing. I wanted Mom to myself.

Towards the end, Kim got pretty overwhelmed by the personal care. Hannah and I would get mad at her for not changing Mom's diaper or getting her dressed.

But without them, Dad would never have had Mom with him at home for so long. And for this we were grateful.

* Not their real names

Nature Lover

This tree had sweeter sap than the others. We would drink it fresh out of the bucket. We called it "tree juice." It had little bits of bark floating in it.

My mother used to say that she wanted her ashes spread under the sugar maple tree beside the old farmhouse where we lived in Maine.

She also used to say that she wanted to be reincarnated as a maple tree. She felt a strong kinship with trees, especially maples.

It's hard to make sense of the different things she said. Because she didn't really believe in reincarnation. She always said that death was final. This scared me when I was a kid, thinking that someday I would just end. Then she and Dad pointed out that the idea of living forever was just as incomprehensible and terrifying.

Mom loved all of nature: plants, worms, rocks, soil.

She did not seem to feel as separate from it as most people did.

Maybe this meant that she was not as bothered by the idea of just ending; it was what happened to all animals and plants.

94

When Mom got sick, many years had passed since we drank tree juice.

One day there was a wasp on the front porch.

It was crawling along in front of Mom.

She reached her foot out and stepped on the wasp, then ground her foot back and forth, back and forth.

She didn't stop until the wasp was a black smear.

I caught myself wondering what Mom thought of herself.

I realized that part of me believed the real Mom lived somewhere else, unchanging, immortal, observing the new Mom.

Dad built a fence to keep Mom from wandering away and getting lost.

Sometimes she refused to go outside.

She stopped seeing small bits of beauty.

Later, at the end of her life, Dad would wheel Mom outside in her wheelchair and they would sit and listen to the wind in the trees. She liked it, he said.

Once I was on the phone with
Mom and I asked her how she was.
"Like this," she said. Then Dad told
me she had spread apart her thumb
and forefinger while she was saying
it, as if to show me what she meant.

Is That A Banana?

There was this family friend who would drop by sometimes to see Mom.

He liked to ask her questions. She usually couldn't answer them.

What's that you're eating?

So he would rephrase them and talk slower and louder.

Is that a BANANA, Midge?

Eventually he would let it go.

Well, it's good to see you anyway, dear.

Hannah heard this and when she told me we couldn't stop laughing.

After he left, Hannah did a whole routine in his voice.

Is this a SLIPPER, Midge?

Mom laughed. She usually did when Hannah and I acted silly.

It went on for days, with variations.

Is that coffee, Sarah?

Good one!

Is that a shirt you have on, Hannah?

Ah ha ha ha!

Is that a head I see on your shoulders, Sarah?

Could be!

It would have been even funnier if the guy hadn't been one of my parents' only friends who still came around.

Why Are You Depressed?

There was a grease mark on the mirror where she'd press her nose against it and talk to her reflection. It was so funny.

We laughed and laughed and laughed.

One day Mom and I were sitting on the couch together and she said, "Will you marry me?" This is what she would say to Dad when he did something sweet.

You mean Dad, right?

She hated the cold now and wandered around inside all day, carrying things and following the oblivious cat. She would carry the photo of her parents and cry.

One day...

No one sees me.

We see you, Mom.

No! I'm talking to myself! Let people hear you, Midge. Let people see you, Midge.

And another...

I'm not really much of a person right now.

Maybe if I was a kitty.

And another...

Cluck Cluck

Are you a chicken?

No. But I'm kinda cute.

At night she'd lose her glasses and stumble around blindly in her bathrobe until we led her to bed.

A lot of her pyjamas had animals or other cute patterns. I wondered why they made these for adults and why my family bought them for her.

These socks say "chicks with brains."

Who Farted?

Mom, Dad, and I were in the kitchen.
Hannah came in and said, "Ew! Who farted?"
Dad and I both denied it, and accused Hannah of
doing it herself. This went on for a while, until
Mom said in this sweet little voice, "No, I think I did."

We laughed so hard then, all four of us.

Up and Down

No! She won't do anything like it! She hates lipstick!

When Mom had to go up or down the stairs, especially down, she got scared and disoriented. Sometimes she just sat down.

It helped to sing to her. Especially Christmas carols.

Fa la la la la
la la la la!
Just one more step!

When Dad couldn't coax her, he just carried her.

Here we go, Mrs. Migdelpopper.

What is it?

God, Dad! Your back!

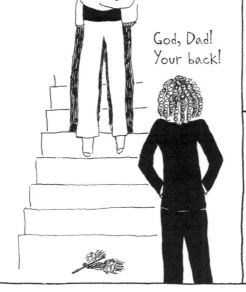

The second floor wasn't ideal for Mom's daily wanderings. Too many doors to get trapped behind and too many corners to get stuck in. But their bedroom was upstairs, and the full bathroom, and the sun porch that had been built after Mom got sick so she would have a nice place to sit.

TV room   Mom and Dad's room

landing   stairs   sun porch

Hannah's old room   my old room

---- wandering

Dad thought maybe he could get Mom one of those motorized chairs that carries people up and down the stairs.

TURBO

Or he might be able to hire his friend's sons to come over and carry her.

Got 'er?   She doesn't!   Yup, let's do this, dude. Don't you worry, Mrs L!

In the end, he decided to move their bedroom downstairs.

Mom would never have to go upstairs by herself again.

The study would become the bedroom. It was a small, sunny room filled with the hundreds of books that they'd collected over the years.

kitchen   study bedroom

porch

bath-
room

The downstairs was much easier for Mom to navigate.

dining room   living room

Mom seemed OK with the move.

That night I gave her a sponge bath. That's what we'd have to do until Dad got the down-stairs bathroom remodelled.

One day after the move, Dad and I were alone in the car, driving through the glittering snow.

I want to keep her at home as long as possible.

Yeah, Dad. I know you do.

We still helped Mom go up and down the stairs sometimes, for a bath or a visit to the sun porch. The rest of the time we kept a baby gate at the bottom of the stairs just in case. But she mostly ignored them.

One day I was sitting at the top of the steps looking down at Mom and Dad.

She doesn't even know who I am, Dad.

Yes, she does. You know who Sarah is, right?

She never answered.

At some point, I don't know when or how or why, Dad had become extremely patient with Mom.

He held her hand and called her little nicknames.

Mom would say "I love you" over and over and he always said it back.

Sometimes they were so deep in their own little tender world that I had to leave them.

One day Mom and I were in the sun porch listening to Aretha Franklin.

♪ Chain Chain Chain ♪ Chain of Fools ♪

Mom introduced me to her music when I was a kid and we both loved it.

I was thinking about how good the sun porch was for Mom.

Then she turned to me and said, "Who are you?"

Your daughter, Sarah.

My answer seemed to stress her out. She turned away and started mumbling and breathing heavily. That was the only time she ever said anything like that. Part of me wondered if she was joking or something.

Phew!

Oh Broccoli, Who Are Simple

Mom, Dad, and I were all sitting at the table. As usual,
Dad and I were trying to get Mom to eat more.

Sarah: Here Mom, it's broccoli from someone's garden!
Mom: Oh broccoli, who are simple!
Sarah: It would make me so happy if you ate this little
bit of food, Mom.
Dad: It's a morsellette. Can a morsel be anything besides food?
Sarah: I don't know. Maybe poetry.

[Pause]

Sarah: So is it only broccoli and carrot sticks now?
Dad: And candy. Midge, man cannot live on bread alone...
Oh, but I don't know about woman.
Sarah: Oh broccoli, who are simple.
Dad: What?
Sarah: Mom said that.
Dad: She did?
Sarah: Dad, you were sitting right here!
Mom: I love it! It's great, like blockers.
Dad: Midge, did you really apostrophize the broccoli?
Sarah: Oh look! Another person. I have one too.
She said that last night.
Dad: What did she say about broccoli again?
Sarah: Oh broccoli, who are simple.
Dad: Well, it is grammatically correct.

Popping Up

When I visited Fredericton the summer after the move, Dad looked more tired than ever. He kept clapping his hand to his forehead and closing his eyes and sighing.

Oy vey

Mom wasn't sleeping much.

Way down south in the YANKETY YANK! A bull-frog jumped from BANK TO BANK, just because he'd nothing better for to do!

Midge! It's the middle of the night! Let's not sing right now, OK?

Dad was relieved and grateful when Debbie, Sukey, Hannah, or I visited and he could get a break from the nighttime routine. He didn't want to hire anyone for evenings or overnights; it felt like too much of an invasion of his and Mom's privacy.

Hannah and I joined forces to keep Mom up as late as possible, hoping it would help her sleep. We'd walk her all around the house.

We brushed her teeth...

waited for her to pee...

and put on her pyjamas.

MMMPH!

Dad had bought a big TV and satellite cable not long after Mom got sick, and by this point he was watching it every night. Someone had to be on duty to keep Mom from standing in front of it.

We'd let Dad sit there...

till he fell asleep.

Then we'd wake him up...

I wasn't sleeping!

and send him to get ready for bed.

While he was in the bathroom, we'd tuck Mom in. Sometimes we'd entertain her.

For she's a jolly good fellow, for she's a jolly good fellow!

For she's a jolly good felloooooow, which nobody can deny!

Sometimes one of us would sleep with Mom so Dad could get a full night's sleep.

On the advice of my parents' doctor, Dad had started giving Mom an Ativan at night to reduce her agitation. He hid it in yoghurt.

He kept the new bedroom very dark.

The first night I slept with Mom I rubbed her feet first to help her relax.

Then I climbed in beside her.

I felt lucky to be able to be so close to her.

For a while she was quiet.

Then she popped up, as Dad called it.

And stayed up.

She sang folk songs.

Well I know where I'm goin, And I know who's goin with me! And I know who I love...

She talked in short bursts.

And Beg pardon? Oh lovely woo-hoo Of course he Hello? yes!

She exhaled explosively.

Phew!

Phew!

I tried to push her back down, but she had abs of steel from being so tense all the time.

Phew!

Jesus

I sang to her.

I modelled deep breathing.

I rubbed her back.

But really there was nothing to do but wait until she fell asleep.

Kitty!

Mom: I'm always scared!
Dad: Even when I hug you?

Accidental

One night I was woken up by a huge crash.

I heard voices downstairs, but then I fell back asleep.

Ow!

Oh sweetie, let me help you up!

When I got up in the morning, Mom had a few scratches on her face. By the evening half her face was bruised and swollen. Dad called from work and told me she had fallen out of bed and smashed her face on the night table.

I was furious. I'd told him a long time ago to get bed rails. I kept taking photos of her face. I couldn't believe it. She looked so bad. I couldn't tell if she noticed the injury. But she seemed sad.

Dad came home with some cheap plastic rails and I yelled at him.

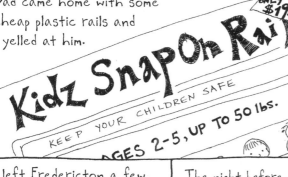

ONLY $19.99

Kidz SnapOn Rails

KEEP YOUR CHILDREN SAFE

AGES 2-5, UP TO 50 lbs.

Stop making such a big deal out of it! These are fine for now. I'll order some better ones this week.

I left Fredericton a few days later.

The night before, I sat with Mom and held her. She seemed so fragile with her bruised face.

After she went to bed, Dad and I talked in the kitchen.

Thanks for everything.

I will.

It's OK, Dad. Just please get some rails, OK?

I left the house around four in the morning. Dad kept thanking me over and over.

As the taxi drove along the river to the airport, the snow got heavier until there was almost no visibility. The driver told me how much he loved driving and how he would stop sometimes to take pictures of beautiful snow formations or rainbows or sunrises. He also took pictures of car accidents and sent them to the paper. He got $40 for every one they printed.

Lighter

After three or four years, Mom didn't know she was sick anymore. This meant that she was happier. She rarely cried or got angry.

they're pretty. they're really beauty beauty!

She often seemed overwhelmed by the beauty of people or animals or flowers.

She sang all the time, everywhere.

my country, tis of thee...

She laughed if you made funny faces.

hee hee

ah mmmm oh and

She liked to pull on people's clothes or bodies. I don't know why.

She loved most of all to pull on Donimo's arm when Donimo was eating dinner.

We started talking about Mom right in front of her all the time, since she didn't seem to notice.

hmm um hmm um mm hmm

BLAH BLAH BLAH BLAH BLAH BLAH BLAH BLAH BLAH

One day during this new, lighter time, Donimo and I brought Mom with us on a walk to the old graveyard. Donimo wanted to take photos.

ANGELINE HUBERT b. 1784 d 1811

OUR FATHER JOSEPH LANE BORN 1797 DIED 1864 REST IN PEACE

REST IN PEACE AND OUR ...

Carlotta Henry BABY GIRL 1814-1817

After we had been there a while, I looked up and saw Mom dancing on the graves, humming a little tune.

DO DO DO Dee Do

AGATHA S. CRESTON LOVING WIFE B. 1802 D. 1827

ANNA MARIE BLAIS 1812 — 1847 IN THE ARMS OF THE LORD

EPHRAIM B. SMITH b 1901 d 1980

Bless he for sh alwa CAROL b 17 d 1

Dad would sing to Mom to get her to take her pills or eat.

"Swallow the yellow brick pill!

Swallow the yellow brick pill!"

Good Grooming

By the time Mom started wearing diapers, she was too out of it to notice or care.

We tried to make sure they didn't stick up out of her pants.

We still took her to the bathroom regularly. The diapers were for overnight and backup during the day. She often sang while she sat.

She was so docile. She submitted to tooth brushing, nose wiping, hair brushing.

She sat on the bench in the new bathroom while we bathed her. We gave her a washcloth to hold.

Often the diaper leaked overnight and we would have to strip all the sheets and the mattress pad. We did laundry almost every day.

There were supplies everywhere.

 soft 'n' fresh

Sometimes I felt like the calmest, most capable nurse.

SARAH

Other times I thought I might throw up from the smell of urine or shit.

Hannah and I decided that it would be easier to keep Mom clean if we trimmed her pubic hair. It was very long. I held Mom in place while Hannah knelt in front of her with the scissors.

hmm hmm hmmm

Hannah finished the trimming.

Then she wiped away the bits of hair.

It reminded me of another time, when Dad and I tried to shave Mom's armpits so she would smell better. She wasn't as sick then, and she got mad.

I couldn't get out of that room fast enough. I kept thinking about how they used to have a secret intimacy between them and how that had been breached forever.

I could never have trimmed Mom's pubic hair. I never touched her between the legs without toilet paper or a washcloth between us.

DYKE!
HA HA

I believe this was partly because I had touched women's bodies for sex, and because sometimes I feared being accused of perversion because of it. That all added to the weirdness of bathing and grooming my own mother in the first place.

When Hannah and I told Dad and Donimo what we had done, they said they thought it was unnecessary. We felt bad then.

You get sick and your body is no longer private.

Even if none of your caretakers ever hurts you, some basic dignity is lost.

Come on, Mom, let's go to the bathroom.

The Great Social Experiment

This is what really happened to my mother: She wasn't really sick at all. One day she was watering her flowers. Dad wasn't home.

There she is!

Hello. Can I help you?

We're from the government.

Oh!

We'd like to talk to you about a top secret project.

We're trying to help people with dementia.

Oh dear.

It's an epidemic. Families are at their wit's end trying to cope.

How sad.

We came to you because you are known for being kind and you have a passion for helping those in need.

Thank you!

We'd like you to pretend to have Alzheimer's so we can study the impact on your family.

What!!!?

It will be hard on them.

But think of all the people you'll be helping.

And... at the end of five years, you and your family members will each get one million dollars!!!

OK. I can give the money to charity.

So she went to acting class...

Great slouching, Midge! And the hat! Nice touch. Try looking a bit more blank. Good!

And hung out in nursing homes...

Note to self: be sure to lose sense of hunger.

And met with her team once a week.

Doctor   Acting coach   Researcher   Therapist

Once the experiment got going, it was very sad for Mom to see us suffer. Sob!

But she would remember the people she was helping and the money and it all seemed worth it.

A few years into Mom's illness I was telling my therapist about this silly story I had made up, kind of laughing at myself. Partway through I realized that part of me really believed it.

Scraps

Sarah: Oh my God!
Mom: (to the tune of Clementine)
Oh my Goddin, oh my Goddin...
Sarah: (laughs)
Mom: Don't. They can't help it if they
don't have enough.

Mom: I say that's little and she can but meanwhile.

Mom: (looking in mirror) This is live.
But it's OK, don't you think?

Sarah: Mom, did you eat the rye cracker?
Mom: No, it's eejier and squiggy to them.

Mom: Something's gonna happen to it.
Nice or not nice, nicely or lovely.

New

In the spring of 2004, Hannah had a baby and named him Zev.

Dad was overjoyed. As for Mom, it seemed like sometimes she caught a glimpse of him, and she'd smile. But mostly she didn't respond to him at all.

I talked to Hannah on the phone when she was up in the middle of the night with Zev.

I miss Mom so much! She would have been happier than anyone else to have a new baby in the family!

In the summer, Donimo and I went to visit.

Oh, how I craved my mother! I looked at her and touched her all the time, trying to soak her into my brain, my heart, my skin.

I rubbed her dry feet with cream.

I tried to untangle her hair.

She didn't touch me back, but she smiled.

Donimo and I didn't really understand the fuss about babies. We preferred our animals.

But we did fall in love with Zev.

We played a game where we flapped his big ears and pretended he could fly.

Mom woke up soaked in urine, in spite of the diaper. Sometimes even her shirt was wet. During the night she would wedge her arm or leg between the mattress and the bed rails and lie there trapped.

She didn't speak much. Her glasses fell off or she pulled them off. Her dark eyes darted like a scared animal's.

Donimo stayed alone with Mom for the first time.

Have a carrot!

Oh Christ!

"Your mom's mind is like the garden this summer," Donimo said.

"Tangled, but with spots of brightness."

Sometimes I craved my mother. Other times I fled her illness and escaped to Zev's new life.

Hello, cute thing!

By this time my mother did not know what a daughter was, or a mother. She had very few words. But in some way she recognized me. My voice and face had some meaning for her.

Come with me, your daughter Sarah.

This one!

I love you!

You're so pretty!

I don't know what the words meant to her, but she sounded like Mom when she said them. And sometimes she made eye contact and held it. Like she knew something.

I finished a short story while I was there.

It has sex in it!

Delicious!

I want to read it to you now, Donimo, while no one else is around.

Huh?

Sarah! Someone is around!

This is the last thing my mother ever said to me...

Do you still love me?

Yes I do. Because you're good.

Donimo and I went back to Vancouver and our lives continued.

Sometimes I was even happy.

Other times I wanted to drive my car into oncoming traffic.

Sometimes I cut myself with a razor, just enough to bleed.

There were days when I felt empty.

Or filled with bitterness.

I dreamt I found my cat hanging from a tree by a leather belt. When I went to cut him down he turned into Mom.

Decision

In July, Dad went away for two weeks and Debbie came to stay with Mom.

Oh my sweet Mirele!

Right before Dad got home, Mom slept for 36 hours. Debbie couldn't wake her up. The doctors thought it could be a reaction to the Clonazepam she took for muscle spasms. But really, no one knew.

When she finally woke up, she couldn't walk.

Just like that. She never walked again.

July 22, 2004
(I wish God would just let her die.) Have I ever written that before? But what of...

Dad spent hours scheduling help, because every transfer took two people.

A few weeks went by. Sometimes Dad called me and held the phone to Mom's mouth and she made noises that could have been meant for me. Maybe.

Dee
Da
Ooo
Mmmm

She spent most of the day sleeping, propped up on the couch so she wouldn't fall over.

One day Mom's diaper leaked on the couch. Dad tried to help her up even though he was alone. She fell and then he fell. He hurt his back.

Neither of them could live like this.

It sounds like you've made your decision, Dad.

Yeah... What do you think?

I think it's completely up to you. It's your call.

I know. But I want you to be part of it.

I think it's the right thing to do.

Yeah.

And so my father started the process for getting Mom into a nursing home.

July 26
It feels OK to think about Dad and be supportive and clear—but Mom—it feels like I'm mentally avoiding eye contact with her or

maybe because a small part of me feels a tiny bit of relief?

I spent a lot of time doing nothing, lying in bed with my cat Oscar.

Or trying to pick fights with Donimo.

I had trouble doing the most basic tasks. I often wondered if I had Alzheimer's too.

I kept going to work because it seemed like that's what people did, even when the world was falling apart.

In August Dad got a call. There was an opening for Mom in a nursing home. It was the one Dad had hoped to get her into: small, with excellent staff. But she had to move in in two days.

AAAAAHHHH!

Dad said he was ready. He described how he was going to rearrange the furniture after Mom was gone. He seemed desperate for freedom.

Hannah wrote that she hoped Dad could wrap this up fast so that she and Dad and Zev could go on the trip they'd planned.

On a trip to Vancouver the year before, Dad had bought a glass egg-shaped sculpture. He had always had to keep it hidden in case Mom broke it. When she stopped walking he put it out on display.

I would get really angry at Hannah and Dad and then wonder if I had any right, since I wasn't there doing the day-to-day.

Sukey came and she and Dad packed up Mom's things.

Wow. I guess she doesn't need much.

No.

Hannah came and brought Zev.

Look, Mom! It's your grandson!

On August 11, six days before her sixtieth birthday, Mom moved into Pine Grove.

Welcome!

Look at all the people today.

I went to work that day.

I kept calling them to see what was happening. They stayed with Mom all day, then went and got dinner, then came back for a while. Then they left.

Donimo and I made a little altar for Mom, with photos and rocks and shells and flowers.

We lit candles and said out loud what we wished for her in this new stage. Mostly we wanted her not to be scared.

Subsiding

Dad visited Mom almost every day.

Well hello again, dear!

Hi Sylvia. Nice to see you.

He'd find her in the common area; the nursing home made sure everyone got up and out of their rooms every day, unless they were sick.

Every day a worker would take the time to do Mom's hair in a neat ponytail or even braids.

She even got regular baths. They used some sort of hoist to get her in. She'd had only showers for so long.

She didn't really talk anymore. Dad brought poetry to read to her, books that had belonged to her in college and still had her notes in the margins.

They both loved e e cummings, even when he was "being fresh" as Mom used to call it.

the Cambridge ladies who live in furnished souls
are unbeautiful and have comfortable minds
(also, with the church's protestant blessings
daughters, unscented shapeless spirited)
they believe in Christ and Longfellow, both dead

They liked his romantic poems too...

when by now and tree by leaf
she laughed his joy she cried his grief
bird by snow and stir by still
anyone's any was all to her

And Robert Frost was Mom's favourite.

then leaf subsides to leaf

Every evening Dad would say good night to Mom and go home. He thought of bringing her with him to see the house and the kitty, but it didn't seem like she would notice. She seemed content where she was.

In the first little while, Mom would smile when Dad arrived.

Then more and more often she would be asleep.

After a month or so, he wasn't sure if she recognized him anymore.

Then one day, he told me, she looked right through him.

She ate less and less. She was less and less responsive.

After she'd been there only a couple months, she got an infection and was too weak to leave her bed.

She rallied for a bit, but then weakened again. No one could say for sure what was wrong.

They said she might not get better.

The End

Early in the morning my phone started ringing.

RING! RING! RING!

Then Donimo's line rang.

BRR-RING!!!

BRR-RING!

ING!

I knew it was some-thing bad. I ran.

RING!

RING!

HELLO? It was Dad. The doctor told him I had to come home right away if I wanted to see Mom before she died.

Dad was sobbing.

I have to go home! Mom's dying!

Oh sweetie! I'm coming too!

The dog began throwing up in the hallway.

We ran around getting everything ready.

Then, after six years of sickness and fear, there was nothing to do but wait.

We left the next morning and got to Fredericton around midnight, as usual.

So we'll go see Mom in the morning?

No. We have to go now.

The woman at the nursing home was my mother but she looked nothing like my mother.

Mommy!

She did not respond to me. Just maybe a tiny movement of her head. Her tongue was dry and brown. She had stopped drinking. The doctors said there was nothing else they could do. Her body was shutting down. We were letting her die.

these things are burned into my brain- red and raw:

Dad told me to kiss her and she would kiss me back. But it was too late. She didn't do that anymore. He told me to spray water in her mouth, but the nurse said not to do that anymore; she could choke. Her eyes would not close. We put a damp cloth on her forehead and sometimes over her eyes. Her mouth never closed either.

Someone had given her a teddy bear. It seemed like all the rooms had afghans and quilts and teddy bears in them. She was so small. I kept patting the body pillow beside her, thinking it was her. I never saw her body again below the neck, except for her hands. Dad said if I squeezed her hand, she would squeeze back. But it was too late for that, too.

we drove away from there back to the house where my mom did not live anymore

I kept thinking about Lucy the kitty and how Mom would never see her again.

Donimo and I, Dad, Hannah, Zev and Debbie's son Erik, Debbie and Sukey. Waiting, waiting, waiting. The house was full of bodies and sadness. It was hard to breathe.

The next day I visited Mom four times.

7:00 AM

10:00 AM

5:00 PM

10:00 PM

This is what I said to her:

I'm here now.

I love you.

You're the best mom ever.

It's OK, um, it's OK... it's OK for you to go.

(Was that a lie?)

During the last visit, Donimo and I waited out in the hall while the capable, kind nurses turned my mother over every hour, then every half hour. We waited again while the night nurse put in a shunt for constant morphine. Morphine helps the body to stop resisting death.

You can go in and see your mom now, dear.

At one point Hannah and Dad were there too. They kept gossiping while we sat with Mom.

Remember that bitchy lady I used to teach with at the other school?

Oh yeah, I remember her. What did she do?

I wanted silence, or some sacred words. But I had just flown in. They'd been there all fall. I didn't say anything.

Mom's roommate Mary kept repeating, "I will! I will!" She sounded so desperate.

I tried to talk to her but it didn't do any good.

Will you help me?

Yes. What do you need?

I will! I will! I will!

We all left around 11:00 PM except Sukey. She said she wanted to stay all night. Cold rain was falling.

Grove Nursing Home

Back in the attic bedroom I took off my clothes and stared at myself in the mirror. I don't know why.

Come to bed, sweetie!

After a long time, I realized what I had to do.

I called a cab to take me back to the nursing home.

We drove through the rain, past the cemetery that was right next to the home.

Sukey was talking to Mom. She said, "Let Mom and Dad and Grandma take you in their arms and go to sleep and be done with it." And she was singing to her, a version of Pete Seeger's Quite Early Morning.

I sat beside Mom for a while.
I drew pictures of her and Sukey.

Then I lay down in the reclining chair and dozed off and on.

Dad picked us up early in the morning and brought us back to the house. A few hours later, Hannah had a strong feeling that she had to go see Mom.

She went alone. She walked all the way, through the snow along the St. John River.

Later... I had just gotten off the phone when it started ringing.

Ring!

Mom's breathing is weird! The nurse said to tell you to come now!

then... everything went very very fast

I told Donimo and Debbie and Sukey to take a cab with the baby. I called Dad on his cell and told him I was coming to get him.

I picked him up outside the hardware store or something.

We rushed to the nursing home.

We did not run to her room though. Maybe we felt embarrassed or weird or something.

Midge!

Mom!

She's dead!

Her face and hands were greenish. Dad tried to close her eyes but they would only close partway. We cried and cried and touched her and stroked her hands and talked to her.

I cut a small lock of hair for everyone. Inside I was screaming.

At one point we all held hands around her bed and said goodbye.

Then I left, because I felt like she wasn't there anymore.

A stranger accosted me and Hannah in the hallway.

Give me a hug!

Who are you?

A volunteer!

Another stranger approached us in the lobby. It seemed like he was going to give us a prize or something.

Hello Hello Good People!

I'm Charlie from the Funeral Home!

Charlie's shiny hearse waited outside for Mom's body.

We all went back to Dad's house.

Shall not want. He

We drank a lot of wine.

beside the still waters.

I read aloud Psalm 23, which was Mom's favourite. Dad told us that. I didn't even know she read the Bible.

me in the paths of righteousness

Then I made two huge batches of chocolate chip cookies.

fear no evil:

There were no chips so I smashed up squares of Baker's chocolate.

comfort me.

We ate all the cookies.

runneth over.

Then I was so drunk I had to lie down under the kitchen table for a while.

Mercy

all the days of my life:

That night I wrapped myself in a shawl I had given Mom, dark blue cotton with a night sky print in white and turquoise.

Donimo and I lay in bed and I felt weird. I noticed the cat sitting on the dresser watching us.

She was so black and it was so dark that I couldn't see any of her features. She leapt down.

I propped myself up and got out my journal, like I had almost every night since my mother got sick.

there will be no more drawing, and I really thought there would be. Mom died today.

for ever.

Next

That night or the next day, some old friends of Mom and Dad's showed up at the door. Dad invited them in for some wine.

Oh, Sarah, I'm so sorry about your mother!

It's too bad you didn't bother visiting while she was still alive!

Oh, we would have. It just always seemed like your Mom and Dad didn't want visitors.

Then I remembered that they had dropped by once. It was late at night. They put a casserole on the front steps, rang the doorbell, and drove away as fast as they could.

SCREECH!

I stomped upstairs. They stayed downstairs and drank Dad's wine unfazed.

That bitch! You told her!

Yeah.

The next day, we started planning the memorial. Debbie wanted more relatives to come and stay at Dad's house.

Ahem.

Debbie, I am sick of cooking and cleaning for everyone! We can't add even more people who don't lift a finger!

Fine. We'll just go back to New York and have our own memorial.

Oh for Christ's sake!

Later I apologized, because there was nothing else to do. We didn't publicize the memorial, because we didn't want people like the casserole droppers to come. In fact, very few of Mom and Dad's old friends ended up being invited.

Hannah made a poster and presented it like a teacher.

MIDGE

Dad read a Robert Frost poem and went through piles of Kleenex.

"once they are bowed/ So low for long, they never right themselves."

I can't remember what I said.

That night I apologized to Dad for yelling at people. "It's OK," he said. "It reminded me of Mom. You have this quality that she had. I always called it RADIANT BITCHINESS. It's a good quality to have."

Frost POEMS

After

Mom did not believe in God.

I wasn't sure if I did or not, and when I did invoke his existence, I was usually angry at him. Sukey and I both reached our limit with him our last night with Mom.

In spite of this, I always knew I would say the mourner's Kaddish for Mom.

In Jewish tradition, you say Kaddish every day for 11 months after the death of a parent. The prayer itself is not about death or mourning. It affirms the mourner's faith in God. It shows that the mourner had good parents who instilled a strong faith that endures through great grief. I didn't care what the words were. I wanted the ritual.

I remembered the mourners who stood to say Kaddish in synagogue. I wanted to remember Mom every day like that.

The mourner says Kaddish surrounded by the congregation, who chime in at certain lines. The first few days of saying Kaddish, Donimo was my congregation. We sat on the floor of the attic and read the transliterated Hebrew together. I wrapped myself in the blanket I had given Mom.

The day after I first said Kaddish, I went running in Odell Park. They didn't keep deer there anymore. As I ran through the empty woods, I felt Mom in the trees. It was as if the air got denser and pressed against me. It only lasted a few seconds. I felt scared and grateful all at once.

Hannah carried Mom's ashes back from the funeral home. After she told me they were very heavy, I couldn't bring myself to hold them. Dad put them in a wooden box on his dresser. He put three amethysts on top for me and him and Hannah.

Donimo and I said Kaddish every night.

Many times a day I was knocked off my feet by the absolute absence of my mother.

126

One day when I was alone in the house, I finally touched the box of ashes.

The air around it felt thick, like in Odell Park.

Dad and I took the toilet seat and the shower chair back to the rental place. We got rid of the bed rails too.

Donimo went home to Vancouver and I said Kaddish alone for the first time.

We packed up the things of Mom's that no one in the family wanted. "I can't believe it's all over," Dad said.

I kept thinking about all the time I spent trying to soak her up when she was alive. How every second had been important.

I said Kaddish. I covered my head and stretched myself out on the floor and cried. I made the Kaddish into my own prayer, my time I spent with her every night.

Every day I mourned the loss of her blazing, protective love.

The words of the Kaddish and the feeling of the cloth against my skin and the solidity of the floor against my forehead comforted me every night.

It helped to think about saying Kaddish for 11 months, and to realize that some day I would say the prayer for my mother for the last time. Each time I said the Kaddish was precious. And some day I wouldn't need to say it anymore.

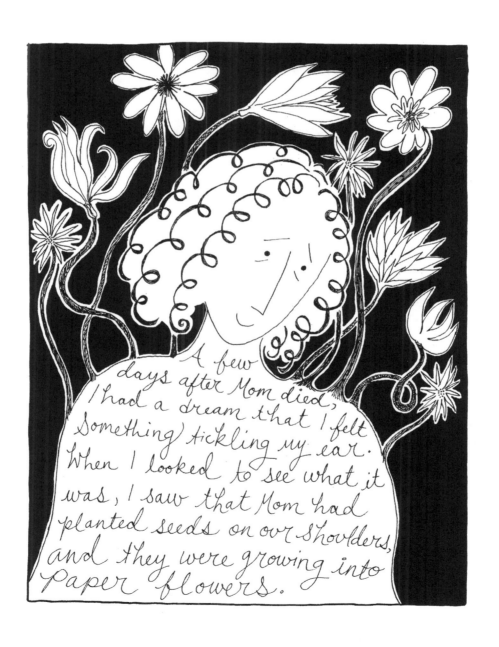

A few days after Mom died, I had a dream that I felt something tickling my ear. When I looked to see what it was, I saw that Mom had planted seeds on our shoulders, and they were growing into paper flowers.

Acknowledgements

I am overwhelmingly grateful to everyone who made this book a reality. Donimo was my rock, my link to sanity, my first reader, and my ass-kicker through the years of Mom's illness and the years of the writing process. My "drawing clinic" partner Mary Schendlinger kept me going with weekly drawing dates, constant encouragement, reality checks, and lots of food. My father Robert patiently and enthusiastically read my traumatic stories about his beloved Midge, and filled in some of the details about my mother's past (of course all errors are my own). Thanks to my agent Samantha Haywood for her excitement about the book, hard work, and determination; Robyn Read and Sarah Ivany at Freehand for their patience, support, and commitment; and the incredible Natalie Olsen of Kisscut Design for polishing my pages into a finished book. Last, but not least, I could not do anything without my wonderful friends, who encourage me, put up with my whining and periods of despair, share my joys, and create the incredible, sparkly, creative community where I live and work.

Sarah Leavitt writes both prose and comics. Her writing has appeared in Geist, The Globe and Mail, Vancouver Review, The Georgia Straight, and Xtra West. Leavitt has written short documentaries for Definitely Not the Opera on CBC Radio, and her non-fiction has appeared in a number of anthologies, including Nobody's Mother (Heritage 2006) and Beyond Forgetting: Poetry and Prose about Alzheimer's Disease (Kent State University Press 2009). She has an MFA in Creative Writing from UBC. Tangles is her first book.

Branch	Date
CN	1/12